**Patty's Story**

*Get Real!*

*Straight Talk
About Drugs*

*By Gilda Berger*

*Photographs
by Barbara Kirk*

*The Millbrook Press
Brookfield, Connecticut*

Library of Congress Cataloging-in-Publication Data

Berger, Gilda.

Patty's story : straight talk about drugs/
by Gilda Berger ; photographs by Barbara Kirk.
p. : col. ill. ; cm. (Get Real!)
Life story of a drug addict who has been rehabilitated.
ISBN 1-878841-04-1
1. Narcotic addicts—Personal narratives.
362.293.   I. Kirk, Barbara.   II. Title.

# *Preface*

I first met "Patty" at a homeless shelter where she was living at the time. It was early one Sunday morning in January 1990. I had come to the shelter as a volunteer, to help prepare and serve breakfast to the shelter's residents.

Patty was seated cross-legged on the over-stuffed couch. The stocky, dark-complexioned young woman was leafing through a magazine. She was dressed neatly in jeans, a loose-fitting sweater, and sneakers. When I entered the room, she looked up but did not speak or smile. Her face was attractive, but she seemed rather solemn.

When breakfast was ready the residents quickly assembled. Patty also took a seat at the long, rectangular table. Another volunteer and I brought out four platters piled high with bacon, scrambled eggs, hash-brown potatoes, and warm toast. As we began to pass the food around the table Patty asked us to stop. In a quiet, yet very firm voice she said, "First we must say grace."

Slightly abashed, we set down the platters as everyone bowed their heads. In the hush that followed, Patty recited the blessing. When she looked up she was smiling broadly and said, "Let's eat."

From her place near the head of the table Patty kept the conversation going. Between bites of food, she questioned us about ourselves. Her manner was easy and familiar. From time to time, she playfully teased a little girl at the table about her manners and talked in a joking way about some of the other volunteers who had prepared breakfast. Her whole face lit up when she made someone laugh.

Suddenly, the table talk grew serious. Patty began to speak about herself. She said that alcohol and other drugs had made her homeless. In a voice hard and bitter, she admitted that drugs had ruined her life.

For a little while no one spoke. Then Patty started to talk again. Sounding a bit more cheerful, she told how things were beginning to turn around for her now. Some people at AA (Alcoholics Anonymous) and NA (Narcotics Anonymous) were helping her get off drugs.

After the meal was over and it was time to leave, Patty walked me to the door. I told her my idea of setting down in book form a true-life account of a drug addict who had turned her life around and was leading a drug-free life. I asked if she would like a chance to help others by telling the story of her addiction and treatment.

Patty was a little skeptical, but definitely interested. We went into the living room and talked some more. After a while, she agreed to work with me on this project. She said she had a few reasons for doing so. First, it would help her to remember what her life had been like when she was on drugs. Second, she hoped her story would help others avoid the mistakes she had made. And finally, she wanted to let those who use drugs know that they are not alone and that they can be helped.

A few days later, we met again at the shelter. This time, Patty told me the story of her life. I made a tape-recording of her account and later wrote it out.

What follows, then, is the absolutely true account of Patty's addiction to alcohol and drugs and her efforts to get straight. Only her name and a few details of her life have been changed to protect her privacy.

It should be noted that although this is Patty's story, drug abuse is not restricted to age, race, or social class. Drug abuse occurs in a wide variety of social environments. Most drug abusers say that their early involvement with drugs was due to situations similar to those described by Patty. However, it is important to recognize that people who use drugs are generally under no greater stresses than those who do not.

*Gilda Berger*
*May 1, 1990*

# *Patty's Story*

I was raised in foster care. I had a very upper middle class upbringing with a strict Catholic background. Materially, I had everything I ever wanted. But it took me a long time to admit this even to myself. It took me time to learn that I didn't love myself. Growing up, I always said to myself, "Why did my mother give me away?"

I went into foster care very early on, from birth. Ironically, I met my real mother when I was eighteen. (I just turned twenty-five New Year's Eve.) And it was with a kind of a regret because everything I was raised not to be, she was.

My mother was twenty-nine when she had me. When I met her I asked her why she hadn't given me up for adoption. She said that, back in those days, adoption wasn't advised. Now it's the reverse. Adoption is a primary issue now.

Like I say, I was raised very nice, positive. Except for my foster father. He sexually abused me. It started when I was seven. And I never really got a chance to tell anyone until I got older. I think that had a great deal to do with my low self-esteem. Like I stated earlier, it took me a while to honestly say that I didn't love myself.

I was in the same foster home, off and on, until seventeen or eighteen. The family had one older son. You know, he was their son. He was a very good brother to me. He was just like a brother should be. He was very nice. He was very attentive. He took me trick or treating because he grew up alone and he always wanted a brother or sister. We were both alone. When I was about seven or eight, it seemed like he was eighteen. He was an adult. He was in high school.

My foster mother took me because she had lost a child. Deep inside, I never felt like a member of the family. Every week I had a worker come to see me. She'd do, you know, intake. "How's this going on? How's that going on?" And I never felt, you know, part of their family. I just felt they were doing it out of sympathy, to be honest.

*Patty's foster family*

Every time I was introduced, I was introduced as, "This is my foster daughter." Never, "This is my daughter." Always, "This is my FOSTER daughter." That kind of made me feel alienated.

My foster mother was very active in the community. She was a Weight Watchers' lecturer. She was in the Rotary Club. She was going to college. And she was very active.

Every time she went out, I dreaded it. Every time the door closed, then mine would open. It started with the fondling. My foster father told me that if I ever said anything, you know, he would kill me.

I knew it wasn't natural. As I got older I knew it wasn't that. Because, see, I was looking at him like, "You're supposed to be my father. This is not right."

Believe it or not, I didn't confront him with it until I was twenty-two. One day I was walking the streets. I was very low, doing very bad, very bad. And I saw him. I asked him for $2 to get something to eat. He says, "No, I don't have any money. But, you want to go some place and be with me?"

It took me all those years but I finally let him have it. I said, "You know, if I knew then what I know now, I'd have you in a whole lot of

*Fear grips young Patty every time the door to her bedroom opens.*

trouble. It wasn't right what you did to me. I looked at you as a father and you're a very sick man.''

It was a relief to get that out. It felt like a load off.

School was a good outlet for me. It was my time to be away from the house. But I wanted to tell my friends. As I was growing up I would see their family units together. And I said, ''I wonder if anyone else is going through this? Am I the only one in the world going through this experience?''

Everyone knew—most of my friends knew—that they were my foster parents. ''Why is your parents' last name one name and your last name another?'' I'd push it to the back of my mind.

I did good in school—except for math. I liked school. I did good, too. In junior high school I started being more active in the school chorus, a cappella choir, you know, things like that.

First of all, I did well in school because I knew that I was always going to be examined or observed. The social workers, they check your school, so I knew I had to do good. Plus I liked school. I really did. I just fooled around a little in school. Made wisecracks.

I was always class comedienne. But I got my grades. So that helped me. If I was just a fool and never got any grades, they wouldn't like that. I would just, like, you know, joke around to break the tension.

It always seemed easy for me to talk to people. Like even when they sent me to the principal, I talked to him like I talked to anybody.

Like I said, my foster parents exposed me to worldly things. I had tap dance. I had ballet. I was 4-H Club. Brownies. Everything a little girl should have.

But I just didn't feel like they loved me. And I didn't love myself at that time. They tried. They really tried. It seemed that I couldn't really talk to my foster mother as I got older. She would talk to me. She'd say, "I love you, here's a stereo. I love you, here's a new bicycle. I love you, here's a leather coat."

But when I was having problems growing up I didn't feel close enough to come and speak to her. Like I said, except for the sexual abuse, the house was very good.

I think there was wrong on my part also. I really gave them hell, you know. "You're not my mother. You're not my father." I was stand-offish. They really did try.

The abuse continued when I got into junior high school. It was always the same routine. He said that if I said anything he would kill me.

I still didn't tell anybody about my father. You know, back in those days, they would tell their parents and it would get back to the house.

As I got older I started withdrawing. So my mother, she sent me to a psychiatrist. I was really giving her a hard time. I really have to admit it. Wouldn't talk to her. Didn't let her touch me. She would try to reach out to me. I'd put up a wall. So she sent me to a psychiatrist to try to talk.

But, you know, I put the wall up for him also. In my viewpoint, you know, psychiatrist meant something was wrong with me. If I wanted to, I could have talked to him and explained. But I just gave him a hard time. "Just because you think I have problems, I'm going to let you think I have problems." That was my attitude. I saw the psychiatrist only a few months.

Deep down inside, my foster mother wanted to know what was wrong, what was the problem. It was very hard, sitting at the dinner table, you know, the three of us. "I know this man. I KNOW this man." It was very rough, very rough.

During the years when I went to high school, my foster mother felt, maybe my problem was that I was alone. Because it was just me there. I was like an only child. Her son was, well, grown.

He would just come in and out—maybe spend the weekend.

So they got three other sisters that needed to be in a home. And that made it worse in my opinion. Because I didn't get all the attention anymore. And I had to share and everything, you know.

The oldest sister, she decided to cut school one day. So for the first time—I'll never forget it—I cut school. And it was so boring. Because everyone's in school, you know. At that time I didn't really have nothing to do. I decided to cut just because she wanted to. It was an experience.

She had some plan to go to some friends' house, but it fell through. Like, their mother was home, or something. So that meant, all day, we were, like, scared because we didn't want our parents to see us. Or the teacher.

And you know, back in those days, a neighbor from three blocks, if they saw you, they would tell your parents. Now, I'm talking, like, a long time ago. People were more concerned. If they saw a little kid getting beat up, they'd call your mother, or something.

Somehow it got home before we did. I guess the routine was to send a cut slip or maybe they called home. I wasn't aware of it at the time. And

I got slapped so hard by my father that I saw stars.

That was another thing. I was disciplined. I guess, nowadays, you'd call it child abuse. But I think it made me a better person. If you did something wrong, you got punished.

Like I said, they tried to raise me right. My father did the beating in the big things. Like, "Wait until your father gets home!" But the minor things, she'd take care of. She would lecture me to death. That was the main thing. My mother would have to be REALLY mad to beat me. Other times my father beat me.

Take, for example, one time when I was younger. I spilled orange soda on their wedding photo album. That burnt him up.

I was just rebellious. Just doing kid things— hiding the report card, breaking something. Because I was alone I'd be cooking, experimenting, going into the basement, getting into things. I really had nothing to do. I guess it was a sign of rebellion, also. Trying to get to her.

As I got older, she'd say I'm too old now for beatings. So I'd get punished. Sometimes, and this would really irritate me, she would lecture me for an hour and I'd think I really got off. And then I'd still get a beating from my father!

And that was what was so hard for me to

accept. Because here he was messing with me, then beating me, too.

My first drink was when my parents—they're from St. Thomas—went on a cruise. They used to go yearly. And every time they went, they'd always leave a friend to watch me in the house— you know, cook for me, clean, send me out.

But this time, I was about sixteen or seventeen. I was old enough to stay home by myself. And I had some friends over. And, see, my parents don't smoke or drink. But they used to keep, like, a cabinet full of liquor.

My parents' friends drank beer and things like that. They'd always have something for their friends—for an anniversary, a cookout, a celebration, something like that. But it wasn't a house of alcoholism.

It was the first freedom for my friends and me. You know, I had the house. I was running it. This was the first time. I only did this because they went away.

I had these friends over. We were playing like grownups. So we made a big pitcher of orange juice. And we had those half-gallons of vodka.

I'll never forget it. You know, we had those tile floors in the kitchen. I got so sick I was like laying on the floor. The room was spinning.

After that I laid off the vodka and started

drinking beer. My friends were drinking. I wanted to fit in. My friends and their boy friends were a little older. They'd go to the store. Then we'd drink together, under the bleachers, or after school, at the store—behind the store.

They were smoking cigarettes. But I didn't like cigarettes, so I didn't try them.

When I was drinking and I'd get drunk, I'd get more happy, more relaxed. I'd tell more jokes, seem to be more at ease. I was, like, the clown. To be honest, I think it was a situation where I'd laugh to keep from crying.

It was like I stated. Each time my foster mother went out, I would dread it. He'd come into my room and it was really rough. He'd just come in.

See, he was like a very timid man. People in the neighborhood wouldn't believe he was doing these things. My foster mother was very aggressive. You know, she's like, "Why are you doing this? What are you doing? Why do you want to do it? You didn't ask me!"

He seemed, like, just meek. Meek and, like, timid. I guess you could say henpecked, because back in those days, he was the kind of man, when he came home he'd give her the check. She gave him his allowance. It was a family structure like that.

He was a foreman in a corrugated box plant. My mother was a homemaker. When she got a little older she went to college. She always instilled in me that a woman's place is NOT in the bedroom or kitchen. I don't know how to cook to this day! "You don't have to cook. Go to college. Work. Save your money. Be somebody. Save yourself. Be somebody."

I didn't date till late. This one guy, I'll never forget, he liked me. This is in high school. And he gave me a little pair of earrings. She took them away. She said I was too young to be accepting gifts. It hurt me.

But you know, this guy was the same guy I drank with. He's the one I invited over when my parents were on the cruise. Him, his brothers, and my friends drank the vodka.

When my parents were there, he'd come over and sit at one end of the couch and I'd sit at the other. They'd let him come over. But I'll be honest with you. I really wasn't sexually active. I was afraid. I knew I didn't want to become pregnant. And I knew I didn't really have anybody.

I always felt alone. Alone. Like nobody, no family. I didn't want to have any problems. I didn't know what they would do if I got pregnant. They were just foster parents. It was not like they had adopted me. And I didn't feel complete. I was sure they'd kick me out of the house.

You know, back in those days, anyway, it was a disgrace to your family if you came home pregnant. Now it's like, "No problem."

The trouble I was having with my father also made for a lack of trusting guys. You know, this guy I was interested in who used to come over—his family, they were alcoholics. Just recently his father died. The guy had already been drinking when I met him.

He was also very timid. He liked to come over to my house to get out of his house, because, over there, they were all yelling and screaming and cursing and fighting and hitting on each other. And he would come over, like, to get away.

But his drinking wasn't as bad as his brother's and mother's and father's. He was already smoking marijuana. I was too scared to smoke pot. I knew if they found out I'd be punished.

I was also a little afraid of the drinking. So I'd try to compose myself before I got home. But my foster mother could smell it a mile away. She confronted me once. She could smell it.

I was sick and I just wanted to go up to my room. But she said, "I know you're drinking now." She sat down and talked to me. I couldn't deny it. I was sick and I was reeking of it. She told me one thing. She says, "Look, your father and I, we don't smoke, we don't drink. I'm going to tell you something. And I don't ever want you to forget: If you're out and you're drinking in a bar or something, or at a friend's house, if you have a drink and you leave your drink, leave it there." Meaning, if you step away from your drink, leave it. Don't come back and drink it. And I'll never forget that.

After I recuperated from that vodka, I just went to the beer. You know, like when we went to the movies, we'd have a few beers—stuff like that. In the beginning, because I didn't know my intake, I just kept drinking and drinking, not knowing what I was going to feel. Misery!

Mostly in high school I was drinking less than the other kids. Because, like I say, my friends and their parents were real alcoholics and they really drank. They were already on their way to alcoholism. They'd just drink it down. Me, it would take slower.

I stopped because I remembered how I felt before. Still, it was the same routine—drink, get drunk, get sick. And I got enough of that. But I enjoyed the feeling. The stimulation. Giddy. Incoherent.

I could have kept my friends, even if I didn't drink. One of the brother's girl friends wasn't drinking. They didn't, like, nag me to drink. No pressure either way. I drank because I liked the reaction. It made me feel more relaxed. It made me unwind, I guess, block out what was going on at home. I dreaded going home.

After graduation I had to leave home. In those days—I don't know if it's still the same—at age eighteen the Department of Social Service gave you three choices: Go to college, go to the armed forces, or be on your own. So I chose college. You see, my time was up with my foster parents. So I chose college.

I really wanted to take communications. But my college didn't offer communications. So I took political science. There it was, FREEDOM! Real freedom. I lived on campus because my time was up. I was like on my own. I felt like I was growing up.

My foster parents hadn't really loved me. They were just doing it out of sympathy. At eighteen you're grown. I was glad to leave. The abuse had stopped by then. It stopped, I'd say, about seventeen, just before I got out of high school.

I think it stopped because of my brother's girl friend. He had one girl friend he was really close with. She was like a sister to me. She'd come get me, take me to concerts. Do, like, sisterly things. She would have me over her house. We would drink beer and everything. I think my foster parents asked her to be, like, a little more attentive to me because they knew I was kind of withdrawn.

And I confided in her. She told me that my foster father had approached her also. So I think she told my brother. And I think maybe he spoke to my foster father. She was the only one I confided in.

In college, I felt free. I drank beer. And more beer. Rhine wine, too. That's where I learned to drink Rhine wine, at college.

Because you see I lived in the suburbs, I didn't know anything about the city [New York City]. The only thing I knew about the city was that my parents would take me to see the Rockettes at Radio City. Penn Station, I knew. If you ever get in a jam, go to Penn Station. St. Patrick's Cathedral. The landmarks, that's all I knew.

At college I met people from Brooklyn, the Bronx. These people, you know, were citywise. I was like laid back, suburbia. I didn't know anything about the city. Most of them didn't know anything about the suburbs. So then I met people from California, Maine, Buffalo—people from all over.

My roommate, she was, like, a mousey type.

*College means drinking and partying to Patty,*
*who is not used to the freedom.*

Then I met this crowd. We were all in the same classes. The school had a rathskellar where we had beer and parties. And I *liked* that.

I think it was too much freedom, at that time, for me to consume. In the beginning I did good. But then more parties, more beer, more sleeping late. Then I said, "I missed that class, I'll make up for it the next day."

I barely made my grades, to be honest with you. I could have done much better. It was my first taste of freedom. And I didn't go wild, wild. But I enjoyed it. It was much cleaner than the drug scene that came later.

After the semester, school closes down. You have to come home. So I was placed into a temporary home, like a foster home setting. I didn't have anywhere else to go.

I didn't want to go back to my own home. I could have. But I thought I knew it all then. Grown. Drinking beer. College. Education.

The house I went to was like a regular home. The food was there. You had a time to come in, to be there. It was in a bad area.

The owner was an older woman. She tried. But her daughter was really giving her problems. I didn't know it at that time, but her daughter was into heroin. So she was, like, coming in and going out. No family unit at all. Just a place to sleep.

That's when I went and started my security job—
my store detective job.

And the more I'd work and bring my things
home, the more her daughter would steal. I used
to get great big bottles of Tabu perfume, nice
blouses, a tape recorder. Everything she stole.
And her mother would say, "No. Carolyn, she
don't do nothing wrong." She'd always defend
her. She knew what she was doing, and maybe
she didn't want us to know. I hurried up and got
out of there.

And that's when I started finding rooms and
living on my own. I got into the work force. I
liked it. So I never went back to school. I liked
bringing home a check every week. And I liked
the power and authority of my position.

In my free time, after work, I loved music.
I had every record, every song and tape. I spent
my money on TV, stereo, and drinking.

I was still drinking, like, on the weekends.
I'd go to a bar. I'd meet different people. I got
close to a friend of mine. And I'd go over his
house and I'd bring two six-packs of Heineken's.
And that's when I'd smoke a little reefer, marijuana. He was smoking pot. That's how I got into
it.

We'd watch TV. He was, like, a good friend.
Him, I could explain everything to. My whole

life. He was very attentive, a very nice guy. He'd cook. He liked to cook. We'd watch movies and things like that. And talk.

He had a girl friend. But she was, like, a negative girl. No one understood our friendship. We were very close friends.

I smoked pot with him for the first time. I didn't have to be afraid any more. I felt safer with him. I knew he'd look out for me. If I got sick or anything, he'd look out for me.

My first experience with pot was funny. I coughed after smoking. Then I wanted to eat everything in the house. Everything was funny. Things looked different. The grass seemed greener. An illusion, I guess. I liked the combination of smoking marijuana and drinking beer.

And we'd drink rum and coke. That's because I found out that vodka made me violent. I just got real nasty verbally: "What did you say? Why did you say that? Wanna fight?"

So, I learned then not to touch vodka. I went on to rum. Rum had a different effect. I don't know why that is.

I met his friends. We'd smoke. We'd go into the city. Then he met a girl. She later married him and they had a child.

You know, I met all of his friends. At that time we were just smoking marijuana and drinking, sitting around, watching VCR tapes, things like that. Laughing.

I was, like, lonely and looking for someone to be with. Looking for friends. Like, he had his friends. Sometimes he wouldn't be home. Like, he was with his friends or his girl friend.

You know, I'd just live for Friday night. Get all dressed up. Put on a new outfit. Same thing. Get drunk. Try to be happy. Go home and be sick.

But then what broke me out of the bar scene is this. Like, I'd spend a great deal of my paycheck there, you know. The people that owned the bar, they knew me. But they really made me feel like nothing.

I would come there sometimes with no money or low money and I'd say, "Buy me a drink today. Can you buy me a drink?"

"Oh, no. I can't buy you a drink."

I mean, "How can you *not* buy me a drink? You own the bar. I spend all my money here." And I realized that they only liked me when I had money.

One other thing helped me to give up on the bar scene. It was that every weekend you'd go through the same thing. The same guy coming up to you: "I *sure* would like to be with you." The

*The bar scene*

same ones begging you for a dollar. You know, it's the same routine.

And I was, like: "Why am I spending my money with you here? I have all these records in my house. I can have my friends over."

Like I said, it really hurt me. It really made me feel belittled. I'd spend all my money and then I'd go in there with no money one day, and they can't buy me a drink.

This happened quite a few times and I learned. And I said, "When am I going to wake up? You know it's just a business to them." So now, even to this day, I stroll in there, say "Hi!," and run right out.

Mainly, like I said, for my social life I just stuck with my friend. He had a car. And, like, I'd meet his cousin and his friends. And me and him and his girl friend—future wife—were really close. And then they had a baby.

And since I had no family, we were like family. I would even introduce him as my brother. And he would introduce me as his sister. That's how close we were.

But anything I do, I usually overdo it when I'm into something. It's like a new toy. Up until then, it was just beer and occasional marijuana and liquor, gin and rum, things like that. Then I was introduced to crack.

But that's after I got raped. This happened two years ago.

The rape happened when I was employed in an agency where at night I was cleaning buses. Sometime we'd get home late because these buses go to Atlantic City. So sometimes they don't come home till late. It's a four-hour ride, I believe, coming from Atlantic City.

So, I couldn't leave until that bus was clean because it had to go back in the morning. And, in the area in which I was walking home, I had to, like, cross train tracks. And that's where the attack took place.

I was alone. It was a terrible experience. I was grabbed from the back. Punched in my face. He had a knife. Said if I screamed, he'd cut my throat. He beat me up, raped me, and left me.

I saw his face, but I didn't know him. I told the people where I was working at. I never went to the police. At that time I felt they really wouldn't do anything—you know, black female—to be honest with you.

I got pregnant from that rape. When I was pregnant I lost everything. I didn't go for an abortion because that's how I was raised. We don't believe in abortion. Strict Catholic upbringing.

I started smoking the crack. And that was about the biggest downfall of my life.

A friend of mine, he used to come to my apartment. He was, like, a good friend also. He was a friend from childhood. I knew his family anyways. And he'd have his friends. He was going to college in Maryland. He died two years ago. From crack. He was only twenty-two.

I didn't know at first what they were doing. He'd always come to my apartment. I'd just let them in. Then I found out what they were doing. They were going through the process of cooking the cocaine and smoking it. In the beginning, I'd say, "Just clean up the house when you leave and let me know when you go." This was because I was a store detective at night and I was doing my job.

He would come and go every Wednesday, like clockwork. At first I'd say, like, "I am not going to indulge in this." At that time, it was in the news about how Richard Pryor was freebasing and burned his face up. That's all I knew about freebasing, smoking crack. I said, "I don't want that to happen to me!" So I didn't do it.

Then, like I said, I became pregnant. I just felt low one day and I tried it. The first time I used crack I saw my friend doing it. So I tried it. I was low. All of a sudden I didn't care about paying the rent. I didn't care. And then the people I was around said, "Yeah, c'mon, let's smoke

*Crack changes Patty's life forever.*

some more crack.'' I was looking for comfort, I guess.

Then my first child was born. She was in foster care for that first year. You know, I was like, ''I don't want my child to go through the same routine I went through.''

I would come visit my daughter. Because I was very confused, I didn't know what to do. She was a very pretty little girl, but very standoffish. She didn't look like me. But I was like, ''This is my first child.'' It was like the experience of carrying a body, a person—giving birth. It was a chance of something being mine.

During the time of my visitations, I was doing really bad. I was into the crack. Trying to pick myself up. I started going down.

Half of these people I was dealing with, they were homeless. They were on crack. They were far more advanced than me. They were coming to my house and using my facilities.

That's when I started getting public assistance. I had a lot of free time because I wasn't working. When I'd get my little money, I'd start smoking. My friends would come by. They would just use it as a place to stay, to be honest. And when you have money, they're your friends. Then when the money is gone, they're gone. It took me a while to realize that.

Being that I was smoking the crack then, I met more and more people smoking crack. People that I KNEW, I didn't know were smoking crack. "Can I get high, too? Yeah, you can come over. Need a place to get high? Come on over."

I always felt alone. That's my main thing. I felt alone. And I like to be around people. I like to hear other voices besides myself. I thought they were my friends. They turned out not to be my friends.

My friend—the one that I told you we were close—I stopped being around him. I stopped being around everybody. I got into a whole new group. Just losers, that's the best way to put it. Losers.

I was not working, not doing anything. I was living for crack. I lost my home about five or six months after the baby was born. I was homeless, walking the streets, sleeping in cars, stealing money. Anything I could do for crack. That's all I lived for at that time.

Most of the time I was just bumming. I would use false addresses to receive a check from Social Service, because I was homeless. I'd go to someone's house and say, "Look, I'll give you $50 on the first, if you let me use your address. You know, say that I'm living here, that you're going to rent me a room."

*Patty finds temporary shelter*
*in an unlocked car.*

Now, I know I'm going to get a check for $350. So $50 is nothing. I'd get the check and I'd abuse it. The check would last a day or two days.

I was getting kind of selfish, I guess. So I'd get a motel room for maybe two days. This way I could wash, sleep peacefully, and smoke my crack in privacy.

I had even stopped visiting my daughter for a while. I really went down. And then when I did go back for the visitations, one day they said, "Look, you gotta make up your mind. You disappear for a while, we don't know what happened, blah, blah, blah."

So I said, "Okay, forget it. I'll sign the papers. Put her up for adoption. This way she can get in a home and stay without having to move around. She'll feel in a family unit."

And they just snatched her away. They took her. And that hurt. The way they did it was very cold.

It took me a year to make that decision. This is a part of me. It was very hard—a difficult decision.

After that, I just didn't care. I'd sleep in any car that I thought was safe or in abandoned buildings. It was during the summertime. A typical day: I'd stay up all night, walking the streets, looking for somebody or waiting for somebody, you know. People nowadays that smoke crack are not just people that are bums. You have business people that smoke. Married people.

For a while, I did like other people did. Someone I didn't know, they'd give me $20 to get the drug. I wouldn't come back.

That's when I decided to change. I said, "Someone's going to kill me! They're going to find me dead somewheres."

So I said, "I'll change over. Be a GOOD crackhead. Run, go get it like the wind, and come right back."

I'd be in one area—a drug-infested area—and certain people would come look for me. I knew how to talk, be nice. And I'd take them to go get their drugs. And they'd give me a little drugs or money.

This was during the real downfall. I'd stay up all night in this drug-infested area. I'd have the utensils that they'd use to smoke the crack. Having the utensils to smoke out of helped a lot, too. A lot of people don't want their wives or husbands to know. They just go out and get high. They'd use it. And they'd share it with me.

Or, like I say, they'd look for me because I was honest. I was the honest one. Everybody else they'd give money to go get their drugs, they'd leave and never come back. I was the good crackhead. The Good Samaritan!

During daylight the pace would slow down a lot. No more people would come. So I'd leave. Find a car or a building. Or go to a friend's house who maybe would let me stay there. Sleep until about four or five or six. Till it's dark. Then start all over, walking the streets.

Sometimes I'd go to a free lunch. It's a good thing they have free lunch programs or a lot of people would be dead. Because you don't want to eat.

You don't have any money. You could have $50, but you'd spend $50 on crack instead of spending a dollar or two to get a soda and a cheeseburger. Crack's a very addictive drug.

Finally, I was going with a guy—he was a cocaine dealer. So then I had access to it. This is like going a little more upper [class]. I had access to it. I didn't have to steal or walk the streets or wait for people.

Then I got pregnant. I didn't seek any pre-natal care. And I was still smoking with the guy who had access. He was the father. I didn't sleep with anybody else.

Then one day I woke up in a car and I said, "Come on, you got to get yourself together. You're pregnant. You got to do something."

*Patty waits to meet with a drug dealer in an abandoned New York City building.*

So I went to Social Service. They sent me to a house where the lady was, like, very money hungry. She had, like, five girls in one room, just to get the money. You had a curfew.

I met a friend there that I knew from the streets. We never talked, you know, but being active in that area, you see people.

I had stopped smoking because I knew I was pregnant. And I heard this new thing: that if your child is found with crack in its system, they would take the baby from you.

So I had made an appointment for prenatal care. But I didn't know how far I was. I carried small. I was like thinking I was six, seven months. Not nine.

I was doing good. I had stopped. I was getting myself together. But then I went out with this girl who was living in the house. She got some money and we went to the drug-infested area which I used to go to.

I went up there with her—a bad influence. I smoked, even though I had stopped for a couple of months. I didn't know how far along I was. We smoked. But I didn't smoke a whole lot, like I used to.

She left me. I'm standing there all alone. Then that night, I went into labor. So I went to the hospital. August 2 I had my daughter.

*Patty's second pregnancy makes her rethink what she's doing with her life.*

They asked me, "Did you use any drugs?"
And I told them, "Yes."

Then I went through the process, the legal
aspect of it, which I'm going through now. But,
see, my daughter, thank God, was born healthy.
Just a little toxic. Because I really didn't smoke
full-term.

So they filed a petition on me for negligence.
Each couple of months I had to go to court. They
checked my background. And they saw that I
usually worked—stuff like that.

Everyone's in my corner. My lawyer. The
judge. And it looks good. I'll be getting my
daughter back in about three months. See, I vol-
untarily signed her over. They didn't take her.
Until I get myself together, she's in a foster home.

Very ironic. As a matter of fact, she's in the
same home as her sister. My worker didn't want
to tell me that. My lawyer told me that.

I don't want to have any more children. So
I was thinking this. Since I'm working to get my
second daughter back, maybe I'll try to get them
both back. That way she doesn't grow up alone.
They're both in the same house. She [the first
child] just turned three yesterday.

I was thinking of going to get the both of
them back because they are sisters. I feel like I've
grown a bit and I really don't want my daughter

to experience what I did, growing up alone, not having anybody.

When I was on the streets, being homeless, I had nobody. These girls can go to their mother's house. They can go to their father's house. They can go to their uncle's house. Their sister-in-law. I had nobody. You go to a guy four o'clock in the morning. He says, "Want to go to my house and get high? You need a place to sleep?"

You're hungry. You want to wash up. "Yeah, I'll go."

He wants to have sex. You don't. He says, "Get out!" And it's four o'clock in the morning. Where are you going to go?

I don't want my daughter ever to have to go through that—having nobody to turn to, nobody to have to ask for something.

Things started turning around for me on August 2, when I had my daughter. I was going to give her up. I was confused. But I said, "I'm not going through this again." I used to go regular to feed her. And I made the decision I was going to go to court and request my daughter back.

In the hospital I decided it's time for me to grow up. Make something out of my life. I'm not giving this one up. At the hospital they were very attentive, very helpful. They seemed to like me.

The nurses were very nice. Everyone, the

whole staff, were really great, even though I had made a mistake. And I kept telling them I had made a mistake. But I wanted to rectify it.

Everywhere I go, I've got people in my corner. They help me. Like, "Come on, get yourself together. You seem to be intelligent. You've got a beautiful little daughter." Which she is.

Like I said, I just got fed up. I was tired. I was really tired of the people that I knew looking at me as if to say, "Get yourself together." You could see it in their faces, you know. Walking around all day, nothing to do, the same clothes on, not being able to wash up. Like people not wanting you in their house because everyone has a bad illusion of the crackhead, which is nine times out of ten correct.

After the hospital, I went back to this house the DSS [Department of Social Services] had sent me to. You know, the lady with the five girls. Being as I had no family, she went to court with me. She was a character reference because she knew I was starting to be drug free. I didn't know she was going to do this. But she offered to be like a foster parent to my daughter.

So they put us in the same house. But we were in different rooms. She had fiscal custody and I had custody. I still don't understand what that means. To make a long story short, it was a situation of fatal attraction. She has her three daughters.

I say, "Can I hold my daughter?"

"No, what do you want to hold her for? I have her."

"Can I feed her?"

"No, I have it."

"Can I buy her something?"

"No, I have everything taken care of."

I say, "What is this?"

"You don't get up for her. Like, you don't get up at five o'clock when she cries to feed her," she says.

She was working. But she took good care of her. I'm not going to say she didn't.

I was working, too. I had got a job and everything. So I started setting my clock. Five o'clock. Get up. I'd go downstairs. She showed me how to make the formula and everything.

But then she'd say, "Oh, no. I got it." So she'd take the baby and put her in the room with her on the bed. So I went back to court and told them I didn't like this arrangement because I felt alienated. I really did.

"I have fiscal custody," she said.

"But it's my daughter," I said. "All that

means is that I just can't be alone. If I go out with her, you have to be with me.''

So that's when they placed her in foster care. And they put her in the same home as her sister. The foster care system likes to keep families together. Sisters and brothers.

I left the lady's house. But then I had to go to jail for a petty larceny warrant I had from September. This lady, she was fighting in the street and she dropped $60. I picked it up. I saw the money and I picked it up.

So she called the police on me. And they gave me an appearance ticket. I never went because I started doing good. I forgot all about it.

Then one day I was having a disagreement with someone in the street. The police came to break it up. They asked my name and sent it to the computer.

I didn't mind. It was something to get over with, since I was starting new. But then, too, that was a bad experience. I felt lonely again. No one went there to visit me.

I was in jail thirty days on a bench warrant. I was placed in the annex—freer atmosphere, like a big gymnasium. Everything is sectioned off. You're not literally behind the bars.

Everybody you can imagine was there.

*Patty is arrested for petty larceny.*

Everybody had a drug background, doing drugs, selling drugs, being in a drug raid. Everything is drugs. They had the woman in there that killed her baby in Pathmark [Supermarket].

Some of everything is in there. I knew almost everybody in there from the streets, from when I was active. See, what happened was, a great deal of them were in this drug-infested area. The police have raids. They'd go in there. They'd be watching these people when they're selling. Or they're selling for someone. And either I used to buy the drugs from them or they'd go with me to bring the drugs to someone.

So mainly a lot of them were in there for that. And they're going to be in there for a while.

I was scared. I was thinking I'm going to miss my court date. And, like I said, I really felt lonely. Nobody to come visit me. No one to bring me money or anything.

In a way, I was glad I was getting it over with. I don't have to keep looking over my shoulder. Start the new year fresh. That's how I looked at it.

One time my friend came to see his daughter. He's still active. I don't want to be around him. I don't want to be influenced.

See, crack is a very addictive drug. As long

as you don't take it, you don't want it. There's no such thing as, "You can smoke it one time and put it down." I got off it because I looked at myself and I said, "I want my daughter."

In my life it's like this: You've been on a desert for two weeks, starving. And you walk up on someone who's having a nice steak dinner. They only give you a corner. A little piece of a steak. You're going to want more, right?

But if you pass them by, you'll never know what you missed. Crack is like that. Once you consume it, then you start.

I had no withdrawal when I got off it. My daughter was a great incentive. It's really a mind thing. It's up to you, if you really want to get off it.

I'll be honest with you. I prayed to God. I said, "Please take this taste away from me, this taste of wanting the crack."

And it's been helpful. So now I'm actively into counseling. I enrolled in this program. I see a counselor. And I go every night to NA [Narcotics Anonymous] meetings, DA [Drugs Anonymous] meetings, and AA [Alcoholics Anonymous] meetings.

I have a sponsor from the meetings. She helps a lot. Speaking with a sponsor, you feel more at ease. She works for the Post Office. She's

*Patty meets with her sponsor and gets some reassurance and support.*

thirty-eight and very, very attentive, very intelligent. She calls me every day. "How's your day? What did you do?"

She gives me passages to read in my book. She's like a teacher, a friend, a confidante. A sponsor is someone who has a year, two years, four years, ten years clean time. Part of the program is that after you've got it, to give it to some poor suffering fool that hasn't woken up yet. That keeps the program running fresh.

Every night someone new comes in and we welcome them. We want them to see that there is a better way. Not just drinking and drugging. They say, like, "You think you have a story? You should hear mine."

I have a list of numbers of friends. Everyone's been through the same thing. Some of the stories are even worse than mine. And whenever I feel a little shaky or a little low, or if I'm happy, I call them. It's support. It's love, which I've always been looking for.

With the drugs, I was around losers. They were, like, just take, take, take. "As long as you have the crack, I'm going to be there with you. As long as you have the money, I'm going to be with you. Let's go somewhere. This man has money, let's get his money."

These new people are like, "Okay, come on, let's go to the doctor. Let's go to find out about a job. Let's find an apartment." Something positive.

Before I started the crack, I would get up every day and work and pay my rent. It was nothing. It was, like, no problem.

But on the drug I lost all reality. When you get on that drug it seems like working is the farthest thing from your mind. You know, little simple things, like washing up, you don't even want to do.

I knew what I was supposed to do. I had no excuse. Like I said, I was at a low point when the drug was introduced to me. And I took it. Now I've been off it since August.

I don't mind having gone through the hell I went through, as long as my daughter doesn't have to go through it. That's the main thing.

I know a woman who has six children. She had all of them taken away. She's still active.

It's up to you. It really is. You have to take an overall look at yourself. That's what I did. "Look at you. You know better. Just look at you, sleeping in a car, walking the streets all night. That's no way to live."

And then, too, I just turned twenty-five. I

don't know how much more time I have. But being in the streets, it's terrible. It's very lonely.

I went to jail December 3. I got out January 6. Then I was homeless. I got right in contact with my lawyer. He was, like, "Where were you? Where were you?"

In jail you could only make collect calls. If you can't get in contact with the person you want to, they are not going to accept your call. So everyone's like, "Where were you? We knew something must have been wrong. You didn't go to your court. You haven't visited your daughter. We knew something was wrong because you usually keep your schedule. And you were doing so good."

So I explained to them I had a warrant and I had to go take care of it. So everyone's like, "Okay, good, no problem. Let's regain the ball."

My goals are that I really want to be blessed with adequate housing. I don't want just a room. Like I say, I put faith in a higher power and I believe I'll be blessed with something, something comfortable.

Then I'm going to devote most of my time to my daughter. In three months I'm supposed to get my daughter back. And I'll work at night, if that's possible. It's NOT impossible. I'm going to be working at night, because I'm getting back

*Patty with her younger daughter, whom she hopes to take to live with her soon.*

in touch with the people that know me. They say, like, "I'll help you, I'll help you." When people see you're trying to help yourself, they want to help you.

I'm looking forward to growing with my daughter. I was just called today. I got a factory job starting tomorrow. I'm just glad I got employment. I'm going to take it step by step.

I've gotten my self-esteem back. I'm going to be honest with you. The feeling of someone caring has really helped a great deal. That's why when I leave the meetings, I get a little down. Because, you know, I miss the love that's there. Everyone there has been through the same thing. They really honestly care.

My lawyer says the judge was very impressed with me. When I go in there I'm attentive. I try to act intelligent. I look him straight in his face. Even my lawyer states that a lot of the girls going through this, they have a very negative attitude.

And you know just being here in the shelter, different people that come—you can see their attitude. You can't act like that. You feel humble. You made a mistake. Act like it. Don't be all smart and want to curse somebody out: "Who are you to tell me what to do?" Look, you made the mistake.

In the last weeks, I'd have to say that the shelter helped me the most. Very attentive. Like I say, my whole thing is if I feel someone cares, then I feel a little more strong about myself.

I would never do again what I did, to put that drug inside of my body and carry that baby. And I've seen people to this day who are pregnant and are still smoking. If they only knew what they were doing to their bodies—and to their babies.

I was blessed because I didn't smoke during the whole time. They say crack using can result in birth defects. I showed poor judgment, being influenced.

For anybody—child, adult—they taught it to us in school and it's very true. Don't start. Because one drug leads to another, as you can see. I started with the drinking. Then I went to smoking a reefer. Then I went to crack. I've excluded quite a few other drugs, because I was scared. But the whole bottom line is, just don't do any of it!

# *Hotline Numbers*

Alcoholics Anonymous (AA)
(Look in local Yellow Pages under "Alcoholism")

Alcohol and Drug Referral Hotline
1-800-252-6465

Al-Anon and Alateen
1-800-344-2666

Cocaine Helpline
1-800-662-HELP

NA (Narcotics Anonymous)
(Look in local White Pages under "Narcotics Anonymous")

National Child Abuse Hotline
1-800-422-4453

National Cocaine Hotline
1-800-262-2463

National Council of Child Abuse and Family
1-800-222-2000

National Council on Alcoholism
1-800-NCA-CALL

National Institute of Drug Abuse, Drug Information,
and Treatment
1-800-662-4357

National Runaway Switchboard and Suicide Hotline
1-800-621-4000

PRIDE (Parent Resource Institute and Drug Education)
Drug Information Hotline
1-800-677-7433

# *For More Information*

Al-Anon and Alateen
200 Park Avenue
New York, NY 10016
212-254-7230

Alcoholics Anonymous (AA)
P. O. Box 459
Grand Central Station
New York, NY 10017
212-473-6200

American Council for Drug Education
5820 Hubbard Drive
Rockville, MD 20852
301-294-0600

American Council on Marijuana and
Other Psychoactive Drugs
(ACM)
6193 Executive Blvd.
Rockville, MD 20852
301-294-0600

Drug Enforcement Administration (DEA)
Office of Public Affairs
1405 I Street, NW
Washington, DC 20012
202-633-1000

Narcotics Anonymous (NA)
World Service Office

# About
the Author

Gilda Berger is the noted author of seven books on drugs and drug abuse and numerous other books for young readers on important social issues. Over her distinguished career, she has written for Franklin Watts, Doubleday, E. P. Dutton, and Simon and Schuster. She has a master's degree in special education and has taught in the public schools of New York City and Long Beach, Long Island, as well as in an alternative school setting in Port Washington, New York. Her work in Port Washington included counseling youngsters with drug-related problems.

Ms. Berger's husband is Melvin Berger, a musician and also a writer. They have two daughters, one of whom, Eleanor, works in the publishing industry. The other daughter, Nancy, is a lawyer who specializes in elder law. The Bergers have one grandchild, Benjamin, and live in Great Neck, New York.

Printed
in USA